# Introductory Note

Written Chinese has no alphabet but uses individual characters to stand for syllables or whole words.

Spoken Chinese can vary greatly depending upon the region where it is spoken. All educated Chinese can read, write, and understand the same characters, but they may not be able to understand one another's spoken dialects (speech variations).

Standard Chinese is based on the dialect most commonly used in Northern China. This dialect, called *p'u-t'ung hua*, or common language, by Chinese people and also known as Mandarin, was originally spoken only in the area around Beijing. Now it is the official language of the People's Republic of China and the Republic of China (Taiwan). The pronunciation guide for this book uses Mandarin.

# 1

## — (yee)

China is **one** country with two governments. The People's Republic of China is made up of mainland China and Hai-nan Island, which is in the South China Sea. The Republic of China is made up of the island of Taiwan (Formosa), and three groups of tiny islands in the Formosa Strait. The country has been divided in this way since 1949 when fighting over who was to lead the country resulted in two separate governments. Both governments claim to be the true government of China.

# Count Your Way through
# China

by **Jim Haskins**

**illustrations by Dennis Hockerman**

*To Elisa Beth and the future*

Millbrook Press
A division of Lerner Publishing Group, Inc.
241 First Avenue North
Minneapolis, MN 55401 U.S.A.

For updated reading levels and more information, look up this
title at www.lernerbooks.com.

Library of Congress Cataloging-in-Publication Data

**Haskins, James, 1941-**
  Count your way through China.

  Summary: Presents the numbers one through ten in
Chinese using each number to introduce concepts
about China and Chinese culture.
  ISBN 978-0-87614-302-5 (lib. bdg. : alk. paper)
  ISBN 978-0-87614-486-2 (pbk. : alk. paper)
  ISBN 978-0-7613-5808-4 (eBook)
  1. China — Juvenile literature. [1. China.
2. Counting.]  I. Hockerman, Dennis, ill.  II. Title.
DS706.H39    1987              951              87-5177

Manufactured in the United States of America
26 – PC – 10/1/13

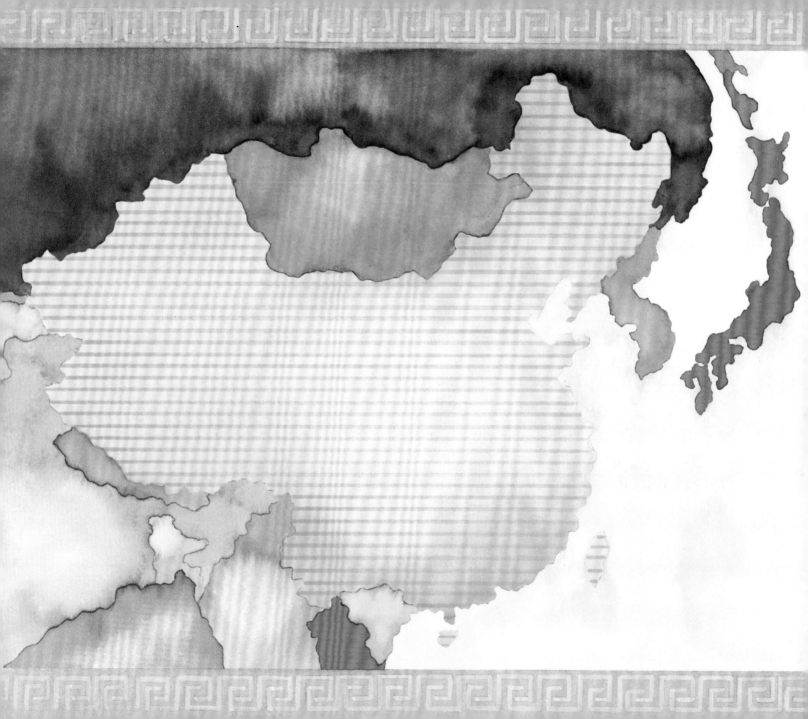

# 2

二 (uhr)

In 1972 the People's Republic of China gave the United States **two** giant pandas. Their names are Ling-Ling and Hsing-Hsing, and they live in the National Zoo in Washington, D.C.

Giant pandas in China live in bamboo forests in the southwestern part of country. Every 100 years, much of this bamboo dies as a natural part of its life cycle. Bamboo is part of the pandas' diet, and in the early 1980s, many pandas in China died because of a lack of this food. In 1984 schoolchildren from the United States donated money to help save the remaining pandas.

# 3

## 三 (sahn)

**Three** Chinese *li* (lee) equal a mile. The Chinese call their famous Great Wall the "10,000 *li* wall," which would make the wall about 3,300 miles long. It twists and turns so much that no one is sure of its exact length.

Workers began to build the Great Wall about 2,500 years ago to keep out invaders from the regions that are now called Mongolia and Manchuria. The wall was built in sections, many of which were linked together around 214 B.C., about 206 years after it was begun. Most of the wall that stands today is the result of rebuilding and repair work that was done several hundred years ago.

四 **4** (suh)

**Four** very important animals in Chinese legend are the dragon, the unicorn, the phoenix, and the tortoise. In the Chinese myth that explains how the world was created, all four animals helped a being named P'an Ku, who spent 18,000 years making the universe. When P'an Ku died, his flesh became the world's soil, his blood its rivers, his sweat the rain, his hair the trees and plants. His left eye turned into the sun, his right into the moon. His breath became the wind, and his voice made thunder.

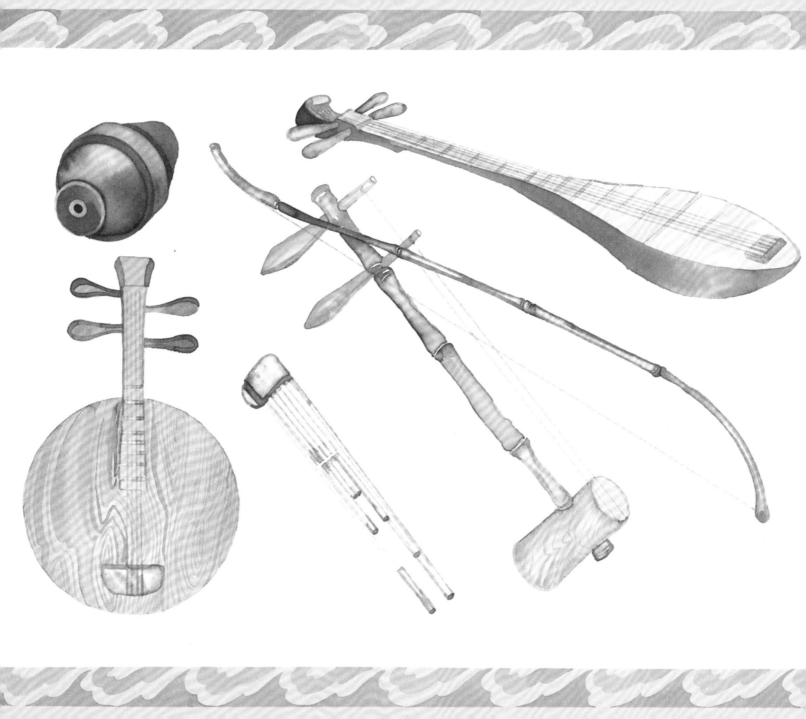

# 5

五 (WOO)

All Chinese music is based on the musical scale of **five** tones. No matter what the instrument, the five-tone scale is the same. By contrast, the music that much of the Western world is familiar with is based on eight tones.

# 6

## 六 (Iyo)

Calligraphy is the art of writing with a brush and ink. Each combination of brush strokes stands for an object or an idea. At one time, Chinese children began learning this art at the age of **six**, but now more and more children write only with pencils and pens.

Traditionally, calligraphy has been closely connected with painting. Chinese artists use the same brush for both art forms, and calligraphy is often used to explain the subject of a painting.

# 七 7 (chee)

China is a huge country. Only Canada and the Soviet Union are larger in size. There are **seven** different zones of vegetation in China. Zones of vegetation are areas that have the right climate and soil to support plants. Because much of western China has a harsh, dry climate, most of the zones of vegetation—and therefore much of China's agriculture—are found in eastern China. Depending on the zone, Chinese farmers grow such crops as tea, cotton, rice, and bananas. The seven zones are:

cold-temperate zone     tropical zone
prairies and steppes     conifer woods
temperate zone     deserts
warm-temperate zone

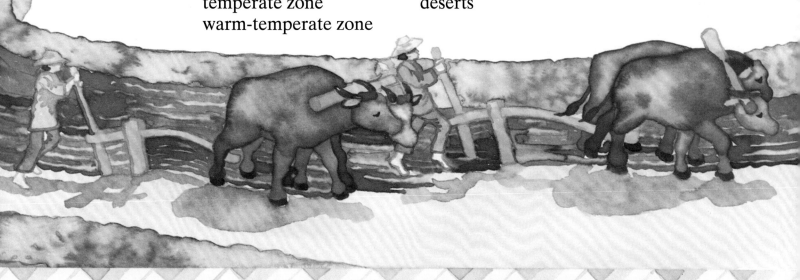

# 8

八 (bah)

The art of making porcelain was developed and perfected in China. By the time the Chinese wrote down the methods of making porcelain, there was enough information to fill **eight** volumes.

Before they were written down, the secrets of porcelain making were so closely guarded that travelers were not allowed to stay overnight in Kingtechen, a town where the emperor's porcelain was made.

Some of the special secrets of making porcelain have been lost over time. One such secret is the art of painting fish, insects, and animals inside bowls and other vessels in such a way that they are visible only when the vessel is filled with liquid.

# 9
## 九 (jo)

A traditional festival that honors the **Nine** Stars of the Plow is held in China every year. According to legend, these stars descend once a year to be honored. In return, the Nine Stars help farmers have a good planting season.

# + 10 (shur)

There were **ten** major dynasties in Chinese history. A dynasty is a family or group that maintains power for several generations.

**1.** The Shang Dynasty (approximately 1766–1122 B.C.) The Chinese were already using the wheel at this time. The Shang people used it to develop horse-drawn war chariots.

**2.** The Chou dynasty (1122–256 B.C.) Confucius, the most famous Chinese philosopher, lived during the Chou dynasty.

**3.** The Ch'in dynasty (221–206 B.C.) A unifed system of writing was developed during this time.

**4.** The Han dynasty (202 B.C.–A.D. 220) The Chinese invented paper during this time.

**5.** The Sui dynasty (581–618) the people of the Sui dynasty were responsible for building the Grand Canal, which linked the Yangtze Valley to northern China.

**6.** The T'ang dynasty (618–907) Porcelain was developed during the T'ang Dynasty.

**7.** The Sung dynasty (960–1279) Acupuncture, which is a method of relieving pain by using needles, was first used during this dynasty.

**8.** The Yuan dynasty (1279–1368) In 1279 the Mongols invaded China from the north. Their leader, Kublai Khan, established the Yuan dynasty.

**9.** The Ming dynasty (1368–1644) This dynasty sent great fleets of ships abroad to engage in trade.

**10.** The Ch'ing dynasty (1644–1912) This was the last Chinese dynasty. The Ch'ing dynasty ended when the emperor was overthrown and a republic (a form of government without a royal leader) was established.

# Pronunciation Guide

1 / 一 / yee
2 / 二 / uhr
3 / 三 / sahn
4 / 四 / suh
5 / 五 / woo
6 / 六 / lyo
7 / 七 / chee
8 / 八 / bah
9 / 九 / jo
10 / 十 / shur